CW01368388

The Book Of Tears

Michael J Wood

ISBN: 9781791976354

Copyright ©2018michaeljwood

Contents   *(All page numbers skilfully hand-crafted)*

Introduction

"But first the ocean" 1

Soft Porn and Romance 15

Travel 37

Memory 43

Human
    Nature
        Tragedy 53

Barbed Wire 69

Morning, Cats, & Coffee 91

Seasons 99

Haiku – A Scattering .... *passim*

Epilogue: Laurel & Hardy
A Prose Poem 109

Acknowledgements

Followers followed
Be like lovers
If they come and go
With no regret
Give thanks for what you've had
Be glad
You've done no harm
And whatever is to come
There will always be the ones
You never forget

Somewhere between the parchment and the pen my heart flies

INTRODUCTION

*"For those upon whom the rain falls
When there's not a cloud in the sky"*

A small handful of years ago now, due to a misalignment of health issues, medication, and stars - or I screwed up, depending on interpretation, I don't mind either way, they all have a place around the spectrum – I found myself revisiting a place of self-medication and alcohol, accompanied by its cognates, depression and alienation. This isn't a blame-game, I've been prone to episodic falls and addictions forever, and I own my culpability. For someone who holds their intellectual capacity in high regard it amounts to little more than act of sheer stupidity.

I'm not the first, nor will I be the last to fall into delusional traps of my own desiring and designing, but it is with unequivocal sorrow, compassion, and sympathy that my heart goes out to those who neither desire nor design yet fall anyway. And so this book is, to a large extent, dedicated to those who, until relatively recently, have been shunned and ignored in their suffering, as well as to resounding cheers for the final acceptance that the Arts and Nature are invaluable to, if not the sine qua non of, sound mental health, indeed to, all-round well-being generally.

#mentalhealthawareness.

Anyhow, the offshot of my own stumble was that my writing came to a dead stop. I was over half-way through the final part of a trilogy that had been moulded around a particular timeline, now somewhat disrupted, and I felt I was drowning in a cold, lonely place. I had to throw out a hand to catch something that might stick like hope.

I'd neglected my Twitter account for some time but, as they say, any port in a storm, so I put back in, slowly mastering the arcane art of the #hashtag which, like all arcane things, is only arcane until it isn't; plumbing springs to mind. I still get an occasional rap on the knuckles for transgressing the protocols but, as I gradually discovered many of the regularly posted #writing #prompts, my world changed (both literally and literarily), and I was, in all conscience, brought back from the brink, a thing for which I will be eternally grateful. And it is a thing, really.

The #haiku tag was the first I used. I was no stranger to the delicate simplicity of the haiku but it was a personal haiku written for me by a visiting Japanese professor at university in the mid-1990s (ably aided and abetted by lubrication - I miss it, I really do, but eventually all addictions take more than they give) that caught me up in its potential for immediacy. The hand-written script in three forms, Japanese, Rōmaji, and English, remains one of my most treasured possessions.

Although the standard 3-line, 5-7-5 syllable structure is outmoded, and always has been as far as I can tell from any reading of classical Japanese exponents, there is a natural rhythm to 17-syllables that translates very well into an English sentence format, and I try to adhere to that rule as much as possible ...

... and I think, within that last phrase is contained, what was for me, the secret of the #prompt being largely instrumental in my quasi- (delusional?) recovery. Whether by extension, truncation, elision, word substitution, rhyme and assonance or not, there is a system of discipline within the given parameters of instant short-form verse or story-telling (in themselves skilful art forms of course) that I find invaluable. Often, the writing sometimes amounts to little more than doggerel just sniffing out 17 syllables, but it can still be useful brain-bone osteopathy. Setting aside a little time to conjure #micropoetry or #tenwordstory is good exercise, and sometimes some themes lend themselves to longer pieces - overall quite inspirational.

The thing about writing is that one will write an awful lot of crap, so a willingness to make an absolute arse of oneself is thereby positively encouraged. It also encourages experiments in forms one may not have considered, for example, #erotica, #romance, #poetry itself even. Write it anyway, without shame, because, anyway, after Shakespeare everything else is mere aspiration. (Just this writer's irrelevant opinion, look what Picasso did for Neo-Classicism).

For me, the holy grail remains The Good Novel, but Fiction is Truth, Poetry is Love and Art, and if you can meld all of those components, you've done it. The very least the #hashtag #prompt can do is assist in that endeavour, but above all is its contribution to salvation, as much as anything else is, that makes it so valuable.

Regarding mental health issues, I hope I empathise fully with those to whom devastation comes as a thunderbolt from Zeus, very sad and deserving of respect and care – and as most classical text, from the Torah to Timbuktu, will tell you, it's not always your fault.

Christmas 2018
(Introduction – Uncorrected Proof)

Hopefully, contained herein, you will find represented my interest in Romanticism, Classicism, Post-Post-Modernist Structuralist Nihilism and other contemporary forms, Love, Philosophy, the Arts and the Natural World, if you don't, it really doesn't matter, but I hope you like at least some of it.

Warning this anthology
contains
remorselessly
repetitive themes
little dreams
sirens seabirds oceans
forests trees
mythologies
and nuts

Michael J Wood

"But first the ocean"

If you sit beside the river when the tide is on the turn, you may see the little rivulets darting in so fast, like pilot fish ahead of a looming whale, to fill the little spaces …

Voyager

Image ©2017 jreedy

... cont'd

Voyager

And every time you lose you win
A tell-tale told me
It's an ocean, comes and goes
And you may dip your toe from sand
Or see the skimmers land
A catch Or dive right in
To swim Or stand
All have their beauties You No duties
To perform Another's whim
Those lips too subtle thin
But some will laugh out loud or smile or grin a grin
That Speaks of tenderness containing Only waiting
For the strings tied to begin Not
Be dismayed of wrecked abandoned
Jetties They're are not yours to moor a hope on
As for every burden An unlading In the end
And even if it's merely touch or sin
There's still a comforting soul within
To hang a hat upon and Linger just that long
Before the carriage carries on
Those coarse-grained friends that never scratch
Sophisticates that turn their backs
And some as blank maps wait to be filled in

> Even fallen leaves
> Have a greeting for the sun
> Wind and wings whisper

Autumn brings its own rewards ...

And all the leaves that fell
That our long nights of chill foretell
Now fade like magic in the land's great swell ...

#Haiku (#Haikuish)

Is sesquipeda
Lian one of the most I
Ronically used words?

        Great days await who
        Wakes to see the sun
        Though clouds
        May try to mystify

In random chances
Flamenco dances timely
Entwined my heart throbs

        Moonrise sweet surprise
        And Sister Sun embrace me
        How the day's begun

Just three coffees in
Already thinking of sin
Guess I'll write it down

#haiku

Place of Refuge

Sparkling shoreline
Tranquillity
Breathe into me
Place of Refuge
Limpid water
Clear to see the ground
My feet might land
A choice of shallows easily
Conceal
A mind for darker deeper
Looking on with envy
At the ships out of the lee
Fill the bottom of my heart
With sedimentary
Rock
To keep me steady on the sea
Or turn my wandering turtle Keel
Over toward mercurial sky
Maybe
To end my days happily
Drowning
Listening to the Siren
Sing her Song to me

Muse

I try to hold the waves
In motion
When I find myself alone
Along these strands
Another year is almost gone And
How darkness sometimes swims
With ocean's deep and secret history
Now the sands run out more quickly
Than the tides can hope to carry
So I play that song again
Of poignancy and piquancy
The one that fills my mind
Whenever birds and leaves fly
Depart the trees
The empty sky behind
And I remember you, my own
But not to own, Erato
If I think of you at all
For it was always All
Touched by a muse
And always will though
Matter little or
Beside you or so far away
I stumble in your shoes

Watercolours

Love the river Beaches
Sand or stony
Foreshore
For sure
Roiling sea
Kissing waves
Crushing rollers
Out of the lee

Water and the colours
It bestows
Waters colour
Sounds into the night
Daring darkness into light
What is caring
If not sharing ...

Light is yet to break
But ripples on the water
Kiss my senses still

#haiku

Autumn Ocean music

Autumn's pale
Unruly disobedient palette
Painting the sky
Up to the troposphere
Salt sea breathes in and out
The Seasons Blue to grey
Like cigarette smoke

Walking out onto another dawn
I take a draught
To watch its transformation
Between my hand and lips
Unexpecting Unselecting
Simplicity conception Simplicity of death
And in between a sea of complication
Simply forgetting

Pale ocean palette
Meets the sky as in a brushstroke
Slash Across the eye
Or in a veil of cloud and mist
Not tears Just
The way it feels with damp and fears
A Winter wind impairs
My stinging vision

I'll take another seat out in the cold
I've seen the Demons in the face of God
And heard the Voice of Angels in the roaring flames
And know I'm not alone
Chill hands Begin to grip
A step, a rock, a grain of sand
A grain of wheat

And all the Stepford Wives are here
And all the Stepford Husbands too
And the ocean renders up their dreams and nightmares
Treasures Traps To seethe
And simmer noisily
And leave
Their winnowing husks Blown
On the arid breeze

And all along
The lonely windswept strand
Will put cold chains around my heart
And try to whisper I belong to them
But still I know
That all the little footprints in the sand
Will tell me
You are not alone

I beached up on a mighty whale
The water rose above my head
Threw me around till I was dead
At least that's where I thought I'd be
She just said Hi
And let me spread upon her back
And took me

Sailing seas as high as mountains
To Talk with fearless
Tireless
Shearwaters
That only ride the skies
And skim the crests
Whose old folks' cries can still recall Amelia
And where she lies
See everything there is to see
Live on a wing

Lines of disparate souls
In difference indistinct
Come Meet my absent friends
Familiar
The desperation Walking
Endless shores Hope and desire
The final flesh to burn Will be
The human heart

And oceans they will have their sway
Everything its time and place
Its love and grace
Its fire and ash and Gaea
My eternal lover
Folding up the rapture Will
Just Simply wash it all away
With one great sweep
Of her caprice and Will
I be so lucky as
To go to that finality
With no secrets

The Book of Tears

Michael J Wood

Soft Porn
And
Romance

15

Perfect Pearl

Like a perfect pearl
It waits enfolded in soft flesh
Until the oyster teased to open
Yields its flesh

Micro Romance

      I tripped and fell
      You picked me up
      Your nimble feet It seemed
      Never skipped a beat
      Just took me in their slipstream

Before the Captain Calls for Wax

The song of Angels
In the roaring flames
Your Siren call
Pulls me to your fire storm
Blaze all around
Consume me

Hands in Grace

In praise of fortune
My two hands
Together
Trace their way down
Barely velvet down
Delicately feel the lines
So sinuously carved
Architectural creation to frame a doorway
Gentle kissing click That slip
To Cover me flirtatiously
Rest upon me graciously
And wrest me out of languor
Ask of me a structural analysis
I will say it rocks
To undermine me from within unto collapse
And I am found distrussed Vanilla
Or Mango Cactus Spice it's all the
Same to me It's ice-cream
Wherever it may melt and stream
And when my soft porn movie plays The pretty
Woman always snores a little
And I will wonder has Niagara turned to glacier
Better laugh at insecurity
And I am slept aside in tidal wave of
Solar butterflies
Spilling warmth and light and air
By flutter of their wings
The happy fortune at their sight Yet chaos reigns
In praise of fortune my two hands
Together Grace

Hands in Grace ©2018 michaeljwood

Angel's Touch/Russian Roulette

Bring on the devil fiddler
Watch me dance the turkey trot
He'll burn his bow strings Long
Before I'll ever drop I'll dance
As long as there's a chance
That mirror-ball of love
Can strike my eyes Touch me
Shimmer me in uncatchable light
Faerie dust tonight
So I may roll and fall
Trip stumble totter reel
Or leap into The black or red
Odds or evens Life's roulette
Is Russian or it's nothing Place a bet
Stack some chips against your beggar
And never be afraid to
Pull the trigger
For it may fire an
Angel's touch Awaiting beauty So passionately
In love And none to share it with
And interlock the shame
Of ardent solitude
To join across a difference of sins
All separation's coupling

Bee Mine

When angels touch they spark and coalesce
Smooth optical tricks light bodies mix
And there's a bee-line runs
To lead me to the flower
In the tree
Would I compare you
On a summer's day
To what
I think not
For every day when you lay
Down beside me
And I feel the warmth of your skin
Feel the stirring in me
Can't wait to swim
Feel your soft waters close around me
A bee mine
Sweet the times I think of you
When you be mine
And there be honey

Colour My World

Caught the early shore today before it slipped away
Beneath a climbing tide Lingering
On the wing
To witness Beauty
Helios' crown arise
Before her laughing eyes
Could break the bond between the sky and stars
Along the borderline That perfect moment
That perfect kiss
Unconcealed
Unforbiddable tryst
Of love and lovers' unapologetic
Loud simplicity
Audacity Where
Sea and Heaven Earth and Air
Make consummate
Then turn away
So unafraid
That they'll not meet and see
And touch and feel Another day

Bloom

Philosophy, romantically entices
Enraptures me So I don't really need to know
Though If a bear shits in the forest
And no-one steps in it Are you really here?
An open question For the clearing
Take on the night, its daemons Walk
The woods in darkness It's the only way
Wasting time away in mining pyrites
Laying money down on Fool's Gold Hallmarked
Cardboard love's Patron Saints
Of Holy Massacres Not sealed with loving kiss
But glue uncompromising Love The chimera
Beast of your imagination And a complex
Fascination thwarted Validation That
If we have luck enough to spend our days in touch and
conversation Count
Us the blessed But when we conjure Unfortunate
Bonds that brook no separation We are cursed
My kith and kin will hold me without blood And never bet
The farm
On love when Cupid couldn't hit a barn door
To lose the fields and trees The canopies
That mottle shadows at my feet Cool me in Midsummer's
heat
And I will hold my petals in until a starry moon come round
again
And Wake me up with spring-like warmth
But never die because you blow me chill winds …

Heat

Do not blame the fire
It is the nature of the flame to burn
To touch but not to feel
Is the only shame

Crave

What makes the moon fall
Will make her rise again
Forgetful or forgiving
Of the cloud
And careless spin
Sufficient unto the night
The tender hot caress
Therein

Love Love Love

Love is such dishonest tract
Of caveats
Fiats
Crazy hats
Too big
That fall before our eyes

I Can Hear You

I can hear you
Hear you like the sea
When you come to me
Out of those infinite shades of blue
And only I can see
Ocean's rhythm surround me
Like an island
And you roll over me
That's when I know
That this must be eternity
In gentle waves
The passion of an aria
When death becomes her destiny
Or Luciano's soul Tells us
No-one's sleeping Nor will we
And all the skies weep
At its dignity
No matter how far we may dive into iniquity ...

Larkspur and Lies

Don't want to keep you
Hold you
Forever
I'm sure you've better things to do
Tell the sky a story
Steal some horses
Ride until the dust describes you
And I'm not going to die for you
If it was you who chose that path
Unless convergence hold us in its grasp
You can live
And die all for yourself
But if we share an afternoon of laughter Skin
And flood As breath comes in
And out a gasp
Until larks purr
And lion flies
And the sun lies down its tired head
Rolls out those weary shoulders
For the last time
Chaos says I love you
Reaching out with icy hands
To clutch a spirit on the run
I'll call myself the fortunate one

Prey

Today I heard
An asteroid burnt up over Botswana
Did it know what to expect
Paint for me my life my days
In monochrome blocks
Complete me primary
Air fire water earth
Come hunt me down elementary
So willingly I'll be your prey
Chase me to the ground
To stop that burning
Before the death I'll pray
For hunger in those wilderness eyes
That flashed as if our stars had crossed before
Paths in the skies
A bush fire to extinguish where
We'll parley no negotiation
Conflagration Consummation I the wishful platter Will
Fight you tooth and nail For satiation
Tear me from my flesh and bones
Those talons rake me over stones
And let the embers take their long sweet time
To cool
Be quenched so slowly

Opposites

Passion True to Art
Must change the world
Tempestuous love the only love
Those rug-scorched coccyges
Elbows and knees
Until they bleed in harmony
Nights burning into days
How ever many suns may fall
Till nothing's left to wet the walls
Laid to wasted All has poured
Love's obligation
Our exquisite devastation And we can breathe again
Not only opposites attract All that matters
How the spirits in our bones may interact
And what remains the soft ash Weary leaves that fell
To hot beds in our gratitude
For nature's grace
To Fly as Pegasus born of Gorgon's blood
Restore reviled Medusa fair
Flayed beheaded and betrayed
By the iniquity of victor's fable history
And Carry back with us sad Echo's
Lost voice from oblivion's reflection
Of her own despair

Pine and Poplar

Is this just woken
Broken slumber
Deep forest by light
Or night In reverie
Scent of Pine and Poplar
Beech and Beast and
Birch and Beelzebub's tree
Breadcrumb trail
Trap for flesh enmesh me
Teeth to close about my breath
Beckoning death
Indecency proposed
Looking up on the end of the world
Excites me more than endless industry
Ennui will break a soul and body
No flies no putrefaction
Down to a lifeless mulch
And when the storms break
And the clouds Will
Break
In the shelter of dreams
The rain still
Gets through
But somehow getting wet
No longer matters

Take My Hand

And if in darkness we collide
Let it be
A rising tide
So many lonely ships adrift
So many swimming in a star-filled sea
But never getting wet
Dark energy
Ever there
Not all to see

We only met
And I don't know you yet
So take my hand take my lips
Lead them to those places you know best
No one to rule, nor fool, no pet
Sometimes the fireflies flit
Across my blinkered eyes
But I don't dare to reach for fear
They'll disappear

Like wispy clouds that race across the sky
Beneath the bullying storms
That drop their sharp and stinging icy spits
So fleeting love will quickly
Free us of the gathering gloom
And we'll not fall from heaven's grace
Our Sybil moon will break her cover to watch over us
Though Karmic irony will catch me
In the end I have no doubt nor any tear

Between the whisper and the ear
Dwells an eternity

Watch the Moon Rise #1

Don't come to find me
Don't try to meet me
If we are on the same path
Eventual Inevitability
If I'm a little early or a little late
I won't miss you
It's just a road, a dusty road, and if you get to breathe you're lucky
Should you Step a little faster
Or Slowly amble Just in case
Dawdle trawl a net to catch the slow unwary
They call it fate And it's infallible Knock you off your path It will
However straight and foot-sure it may seem
As wicked winds that find their way past trees when all the verdure's blown
And if we talk of love The gentlest sweet companion
Shelters me from harsh Aeolian blast
Don't mention crush Beneath the weight Maybe
I'll stand to watch the moon rise You run into me
And willing fall like leaves that brush and spin a tumbling waltz
Along an autumn breeze and
Fall Together ...

Micro-love

    Coal black night
    First dance steps in the fire light
    Whether we tremble or we glide
    Our sinuous slide to sunrise
    Then we'll know

        The summer sun tyrannical
        Bent our backs in passionate labour
        Winter's weak and failing heat
        Threadbare as our worn out love

Can you
Imagine me
And Love
While I talk softly of its torments
And harshly
Of its virtue
She remembers you
From time to time
Shall I put all the parts together
Like dementia's fractured story arcs
Lost somewhere in the stratosphere
I guess she thought
You'd come
To look for her

A Taste of Paradise

While the earth sinks beneath the sun
Sends us spiralling
Vertiginous you and me
Why would I choose Paradise
A throw of dice
That maybe angels welcome me
I've tasted
And the ecstasy
Bend the light and bend the world
Around my tragic expectation
I choose paradise in front of me

And if you come to me

Offering more
Should I say 'when'?
No, I will fall full
Headlong
Willingly
Into that singularity
Lips anticipating
Its soft
Yielding
Vulnerability
Let it run all over me
To be afraid of giving
Is to be afraid of living
It never fills
It only overflows
Deliciously

Crazy for the Sun

I love the way the ocean
Goes crazy for the sun
Tempos of desire
Tumble roll run
Ravenous devotion
Constancy and motion
I love it when our bodies sing
In harmony point and counterpoint
Leitmotif and lyric
Verse and chorus
Sinking swimming
Rhythmic
And then
When
Your jazz heart
Shivers
My spine
With syncopation
Violates my structural
Expectation
Variation always satiation
Happiness
Like long nights
When the music plays

#lovesongs

Let appear a body
Small and fragile
Naked body In dereliction
Of passion
Gives up secrets
Past Over such simplicity
Not those dark benighted of the soul
Just the tracks of history
Fingertips find the nodes
Repaired calcification on the ribs
Those little blank cartouches on the hip
That never darken
Softening of nativity
Sadness in the eyes maybe
Or ectasy and venom In the teeth
And stare of eyes says
Think what the hell you like
She doesn't owe an explanation
And in the urgent and forgetful
Fury Lovemaking doesn't heed
No puzzle to be solved Sheer
Mountainside
A Landscape
To negotiate Carefully
As caution of a precarious goat
Amaze of interlocking spurs into the distance
Far as I can see Infinity

#Haiku-ish Sof-tish

So much soft tissue
Cannot be designed for war
Just dark decadence

Counterpoint Redux

Wake to your soft whispers
Counterpoint
Dawn's breeze
Leitmotif
Fugue state
Flows
All along my grateful consciousness
The music that you play

Don't need to reason
Don't need even
To open my eyes
Feel you glide
Across my skin
To know it's you I'm in

Fairyland

Fairyland luster
Just As
It must be
Conjuring gifts of
Arcane mystery
Exquisitely
Immersive
Enveloping the
Mundane invisibly
Subversive
In its glory
Cast me
A Serpent's eye
Entice and
Mesmerise me
Witch's brewing up a
Secret story

Michael J Wood

Travel

37

A Memory

Once rode the train
From Valencia Spain to Copenhagen
Had to wait over at Cerbère
Cos the tracks didn't meet Then
There
Those incompatibly gauged
French and Spanish railways didn't matter much to me
Where a charming bar and patio tables sat
Beside a tangled mass
Of twisting rails and overhead HV
And the humming of wires and thrumming of steel *chemins*
Sang of distant locomotion
Sat with a beer and a smoke to watch the lemony
Sun Set behind the last high bluff
Of the Pyrénées-Orientales
Before they tumbled into the irresistible
Mediterranean Sea
Had to take The overnight
Montpelier to *Paris*
Shame not to see the landscape
But with luck and an inconvenient gauge
The Cosmos
Synchronicity
I Found myself
Next to a fellow traveller She
A Murakami buff And everything
Was on the same page

Come the rustle in the reeds
Wings spreading for the flight
Take on the air
Which way the dirt road leads

        Oh let this train ride
        Be so slow and rock and roll
        Me till it's over

        Cold light quiet river
        To cleanse my soul like heaven
        At my fingertips

        #haiku

Sacred

How will I ever grow tired of
The river's remorselessly
Gentle roll
To carry every sacred heart
Along its journey
Each eternal soul
And lead it to the ocean
Immemorial
Springs from mountaintop
To paradise immortal strings
To bow before my own
Beloved slowly
To know
Each note
The elegance and rapture
That it sings

Wind and Turn

Such earthly pleasures
And a thousand suns
I've seen
And turned with every one
Between
Worlds I have spun
And still through darkness, storm
For all the winds that run
To catch me
There will never be
A thunder big enough
To stop me
Flying …

Recalling old journeys #haiku

Look for me in Kairos
Where the edge of dream entwines
The living day

Your dreams just turned a
Corner on the unlit road
That seemed to never end

On the cherry road
Searching at my feet for straw
But finding only gold

Michael J Wood

MEMORY

43

A Story of My Life

Dreaming in the dark Of bird-sung creaky sunrise
In the shadows just before the dawn Feel the tremble in the air
The wild dramatic skies will play a tune to guide
No need the puppeteers of Lumiere Unfurnish all the fears
The marionettes must snip their own strings
Take their cue to dance from their own fingertips
The Muses, Fates and Furies will let slip the Stormcock
Glad to give voice Sightless in the Thunder Wind and rain
And Peacock Butterflies will flutter to deceive
While velvet moths of soft combed wings Will
Wait to stroke the moonbeams Who in darkness Still
To burn in candle light Yet Keep the flame close to their heart
And halos round the moon
That burn with cold fire To cool my arching Back in passion
Ring around the moonlight Sweet
Judy Blue Eyes Judy Brown Eyes Oh You've got Grey Eyes
So much Temptation In New Order All the words that ever wrote
The long Deep sounded journey from dystopia to hope My ruby
Throated Little sparrow Croaked Gauloisian
Life so ripe with sadness Glory Ever No regrets
Love the one you're with Steve Still Says Love Can only be the Other

Love, The one you're with The Punctuation marks My life
The places where I care to pause The words have all been spoken
Susie Sun-day told us Other words already in a story This is yours
A history of words in different orders Little dreams sustain us
After all there is a space between us
High-flown birds will dream of peanuts Lunches packed in oyster shells
And love Ah love Can never ask of you what you don't want to
And yet Do Touch your skin my arms so drawn to Never need
Unravelling
Enter in Because you fit And I slip
Underneath your charms Your charity So easily
And I will work my words of clay to throw and turn and sculpt
The shape of melancholy
However high the sky How high the moon
There is a touch that just for you
Even if sometimes it's just a touch of loneliness
Still there will be another tune The shape of synchronicity ...

Archeology

The waters
Rise
Quite suddenly
Love-lust's hurricane
To overwhelm
And inundate me
Those moments broken
That once I thought
Continuity
Such secrets revealed
Made a mockery
Now just remaining shards
Mere archaeology

Archaeology © 2015 michaelwood

Memory

One day I will return to you
The pendant pearl
You left behind last night
But until then
I'll be content
With hot sun sculpted sapphire memory
Skies beyond the fire

Fallen

If I leave my luggage on this bed
A sheet a page
Will it be unpacked by servants Chambermaids
A friend
Someone I'll never know
Folded Dressed and put away in drawers and closets
At the back
Pulled out one day Past dead
To sniff To launder
Send along its way to thrift
Most charitably
No space no time
For those who hear the words not said
Yet hope they hear the words unspoken
On the line
Between the lines lies
No-man's-land
Where friend or foe may meet to play or kill
That land is my land
And I'll cast seeds of what I wish would grow
But I can't halt the reaper or the hoe

Stopping Time

If I could
Would I Stop
The time dissolving
Can time dissolve or just the bones that carry it
Did I dream of being little More than
Seventeen again
And live my life back O To back life
Palindromically A life back
In haiku syllables
And symbols No back story
What use memory
Without forgetfulness And recall
As the flesh falls from my bleaching bones Will I cry
I want to live forever Did I say that once before
All the hurricanes that overwhelmed and inundated me
And I can still recall Every caress and wanton sexual kiss
If I could simply hold the memory
To become a tree Or feed a polar bear made skinny
For lack of nourishment to feed her hungry infant breed
Starved by my imagination Should that not be
Enough for me The Atavistic cell
Memory Of quantum transference between
Now and then
Mere interruption in a roaring solar wind
I am monkey 1-0-1 Now all the guys
The pathfinders are gone But their work
Remains I found in the old offices
Typewriters Rust
And cobwebs
While a thousand monkey bones
Scattered Cross the concrete floor ...

Those Bones

Those bones those dry bones
Will come a-rising up in fond
Forgiving revelry
As some old tender jester
Or haunting mockery
Some fear-filled memory
To curl its cold
and slimy tentacles
Around and round
Impale and pierce and pluck
Your icy heart
Indifferent of your pentacles
To hold above the fire
Until it drip
And sputter burn
As fat upon the spit
Come forth rise up
You skeletons be flesh once more
Come Bless me or possess me
I will remember you
    … just as before

#Halloween

Midnight

Be strongest when the light fails
This will be my midnight song
The one that only leaves to lead me If
There is a line
Around my throat to slit
If I can't see it Will it
Cut at all A fear
Of all the tears that fall
Of all that
Tears my heart my eyes my flesh
If I can't see them can they touch me still
Its mists the trammelled rendezvous
With unseen snags beneath my feet
That make me falter
Never show me teeth
That bite has come from curling lips
Round teeth that bare in secret Known
Antipathies
What frightens me at midnight
Is what daylight shows me
In its garish light to glare my sight
When all of Midnight's mist is merely
Seeing clearly

Muse Me

Kissed by a muse
On sunrise gently carried
Another day
My little luck sustains
To glide across the land
Take my hand
Deep-mining for the words
Unused to being spoken
No shallow pen-stroke tokens
Runes
Out of ruins
Reawoken
Vivid
On your leaves
And when you stoop
To kiss goodnight
Still the impress
Arms
Around
My skin retains
As soft vellum
Another page
Priceless
Of memory

Michael J Wood

Human (and/or) Nature And Tragedy

Of all the bizarre philosophical ideas to be proposed
How often people will select their nature as the valid one
Amidst such a diversity of natures, just as they will select their own
Particular agenda to decide when history begins
From whence all other avenues are closed
Is that which leads us further
Down blind alleys
Everything is connected
To win, to lose
To care not either way
To love and cheat
To lie or cherish, comfort
Choose

The Book of Tears

All in a Day

What signifies
Each drop of ink
The pen, the hand, the heart and soul
To think
Love and heaven-sent reality of thunder
Shame and pain and fluid ecstasy
Seldom intersect so fluently
But when These Unruly elements decide
To collide and mix in magic
Poetry elides Yet
Still regret Forget Some time let
Slip unsteady hand
Some words in jealousy that Make a smudge
A stain indelible upon your palimpsest
But Art will follow find you force you to submit
Or live a life in darkness fit
For nothing but extend it
Past its sell-buy Deity
While Nature's Art of Beauty Deities
All tumble out before you
Like a squirrel bundle seeking fun
In early morning sun
And Nature Art of Beauty serve a purpose
Truth and Truth is Beauty thus
Red and Green and Black and Blue and White
In tooth And claw and gentleness So to the point
The shore the point of destiny ...

Infinity, eternity Meet at the point
And all the liquid splendour of the river Wash away
Old angers' dust

To Walk a long long mile that's only measured by the smile
Along the way Old damaged willow dares to throw another spray
Old damaged man will sit out of the sun but never let time beat him out of being
Some Have been here such a very long time
Still In death as monsters walking Old friends
On new days Stopped and Fell
To talking
The dimples on my heart from tender fingertips
That lent a delicate parasol
To save me from perennial rain
Perpetual ...

All in a Time

Poetry to open up the incarcerate soul
Tormented into twilight early fog
So quiet the trees now
Wait to disrobe
The summer blown
And do I overreach
Arrive too soon
When still there's dawn to burn the sky
To wish for morning's rosy fires
As chill begins to creep
Across the floor
And what will keep
My feet warm
Autumn
Season of embrace
And socks and shawls and memory
And knowing There'll
Be spring again And hungry hobbies on the wing
Return
From arcane African lands
Their secret undiscovered yet I'm told
And there will Be spring again
With sunlight sheen And trees sigh green
And fondness
Full of ice and snow and mist
Upon the breath

Mirror

I am water, black
Baltic black
Icy black
Fearsome gloom
A dark mirror
Looking back
From some Unknown
Dismal room
No reflection
When I'm done
No dissection
Nor deliberation
No redemption
Throw my empty soul
Into perdition's sea
To let the fishes feed upon

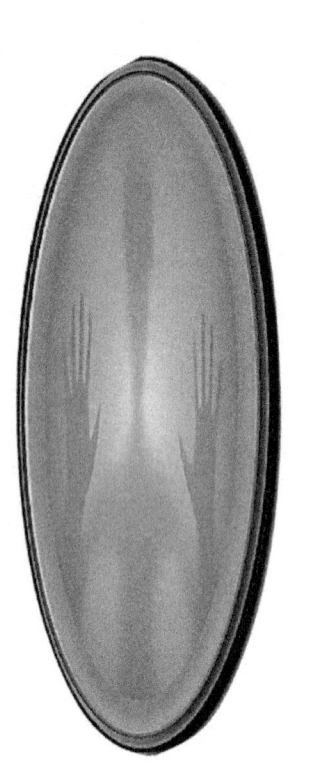

Icarus #Silent Shouting

Icarus, my friend
You have returned from death and dare

    Did you think I went away?

Just to the bottom of the deep deep sea

    Did you think that breathless waves
    Could keep me there
    Hold me down?
    I am idea I am thought
    Imagination revolution
    Reckless bold
    Irreverence rebellion
    And I will not die for you so easily

What will you do?

    I will rise up again
    Drown me in the ocean
    Burn my wings in perpetuity
    And I will cry Yes
    I will weep
    Never ashamed to wipe my eyes
    Flay my flesh into hubristic infamy
    Try and stop me
    Flying Out of the sun

And my ashes choke your unshakeable certainty
Sun shouts through the haze

Seagull shouts for pure delight
Can you fly like me
I'll shout at Mephistopheles
Crash burn rise and fly again into eternity

Jazz – Disturbingly Pretty

He tells me
With utter confidence
Rest assured

Whoever opens up those Pearly Gates they'll be playing jazz
Consider all your options

The heavens played jazz when you scatted my body and soul

Got my first diagnosis of death today
Could take some time Apparently
That's more or less Time
Goes any way it can
Like water It just runs away
You can't save it for another day
Trying not to look
Like the piously improbable
Who only see the world through their third asshole

Valhalla squats
Upon Nirvana's chest

All available flesh and bone
Leaking sex like a Schiele sketch

To demand a reconciliation

And she replies I've moved on
I'm really not here anymore
Only in your imagination

My heart
He replies

Oh no I don't think so That only tocks in time for you
Alone
Or you might have noticed what has gone
That I'm gone
Where there's nowhere near enough space to hold my emptiness

Conquistador

If I struck at every tragedy
Each day there would not be
Sufficient seconds in the cosmos When
The Lennoxes de Paris Invited me
To dream and I saw catapults
And leaping vaults Those Aztec walls
Old Montezuma's Halls
And swords that used to gleam Conquistador
In search of gold* You stole
My heart For the love of God
When it was already destined
For Sacrificial blood
The blade of my own blood-soaked clerisy
Of striking similarity Riddle raddle Plunder me in mines
Whose god shewed me the better times
Synchronic times Synchronic lack of empathy
My diachronic destiny Its sensibility May lead me
To believe that innocence and guilt go only
One way That's to labour in futility
When repetition truly is the crime

Forest Me

Let no reprieve Of power to amaze
Keep from me Forest days
Wonder
What fallen rain
And sunlight
May achieve

Sweet-scent, sweet sent
Leaves And leave to pass by
Undeceiving harmonies
Soliloquies
And symphonies of light
Pour down
Through yielding canopies
On wild And elegantly
Lazy eglantine's Diurnal stars
That shine right back
At Sister Black Night's
Brilliant sparks As it should be

And eyes to see See me
Lost in a dream
A scream of nothingness
To retrieve And
Our abiding legacy To be To stand
And watch it grieve

Forest Path

What the forest path will show
Fills up my senses
So the troubadour once told
More than I could ever know
Will cram my entire soul with
Elder wisdom overflow
And In darkness scratch
The conscious flesh
With shadows real to touch
Night stalkers walk the ground
The air above Yet still in daylight
There abide
With jaws
As grinding dangerous
And large as asteroids
But now outshone
A forest cultivates in darkness and in light
And still the path leads where it goes …

Submerged

Daddy always told me I could soar
I always heard you quietly opening doors
He said
Those dark nights
The picture frames
Always seeking more
Girl he said
You can go anywhere
Float or fly or swim or sink
As deep as your own delight desires
Or your heart wants to dare
For as long as there's air Or
As long as your breath can last
You can sail on violent seas
As easily
As pretty pools
But keep some freeboard
Between you and drowning
It takes a soul to bind a heart
No captive stone across the way
And in the end
Love must love you back
Or it's too high a price to pay

Stranger in Your Valley

I am the deep I am the castaway
I am the strangeness in your valley
The mist that rolls on hills I am
The desperation in your heart
The sudden kiss that makes you start
To want more I Swoop and prey
Like ghouls and vultures
Harriers of the light
I am the magic of the bee
I am the battle and the sting of fiery whiplash
I am magical and I will storm into your life
Or meet you on a dark night
To calm or cause the strife you crave
Conjure your illusions
Diffuse your life's confusion
I have seen your art your artifice
Heard it speak and try to quieten me
But I abide unquenchably
You have no dominion over me

Wavelets

Today's discarded creatures
And the gentle river
That abandoned them
Lapping
Faithless puppy
And disposition to ignore
All of nature
Red in tooth and claw
And all the other colours in her store
Capricious as the Devil's Jaw
And if you lie down with her be sure to know
How her fey vagaries may bring you low ...
And every second worth a lifetime

Michael J Wood

Barbed Wire

If the truth offends
Then put to bed your senses
For it never ends

Barbed Wire #1: Be Strong

In a lonely narrow land somewhere
Between the loving and the missing
There lies existence and the wishing for those tender skies
That don't exhort to staying strong
But wrap their folds of gentleness
Around and lay you on the ground with a caress
To far-off strains of some lost lullaby
To wait for dry eyes

If my tears, my cold starvation, cannot move you
Then motivate yourself to walk away from me
I do not need you at my side
If not compassion nor your empathy
Can stretch to distant discrete frailties we
Who dwell in lucky lands
Not crates in foreign compounds
Not to stand despised with outstretched hands, and
shied away

Have you something then to tell me
Are you here to buy and sell me
Come closer do you smell me
Or does all true sense elude you
In your solipsistic, self-existing dipping-toe delusion
Or is it simply you've forgotten
Just whose side the barbed wire's on

Barbed Wire #2: Serpent

There's a serpent bearing down upon my heart
While I dream of an awakening In darkness
I expect to see the light In light
I ask the shade to hold me up, to keep me standing
To show me where I'm walking And
That's why the moon The morning moon will try to hide me
Ride the river down
Into the sea Where to drown The worm
Before it skewers me
Transfixes me, stab strike and sting me And another
Trace of blood and tear wash into water
Thinned to spiralling wisp
To deliquesce to nothingness
Charcoal mist of night and cotton clouds can fill
My mind with false anticipation
That it were true that velvet cloth surround my dreams
But it's so very coarse the shroud I use to keep me warm
Where I lie Down in winter fields
Where once were days of hay now Gravity Will keep me
Stuck to this old earth, its ridges cold and hard my soul
Imagining
The pebble in my back might be a smithereen Of hope
Sometimes a fug will find me lose me blind me truly Just
A hole I dug with a bottle and a spoon That's why the moon
The Desert moon and runes and catacombs
Where memory wraps it chains around my sorrows
Like Marley's Ghost and binds me to regret

And I have worked so very hard to earn this fearsome loneliness
When kinder idleness had served me better

That's why the moon Deserted moon's
Dispassionate Selene's careless moodiness I wish
A hecatomb My private slaughter of the shadows
My life as Theseus' ship My destiny the wreckage formed
Of parts forgotten, gone forever Some scattered on the shore
And I fall down but I endure
That fugitive peace
Stays out of reach till I come back again

Michael J Wood

Barbed Wire #3: Salt

I adore the absolute
Veracity of dreams and salt
That that false
Friendly sugar
Can't compete
Sugar sweet maybe
Honeyed words drip temptingly
From lips A dizzying romance
Of course We will remember you
Sunshine and salad days
That taste of chalk and salty sea
Like rusted railyards
Marshalling my past
To this tired track

And I'll read out the names of all
The Spartans at Thermopylae
And tell me their addresses
I should like to send a card
Old faros now
Old sentinels
Their cataracted eyes
Left behind to wonder
On a falling tide
A nail
A destiny
And the beacons don't get lit no more
Simulacra of civility
My ship passed in the night

Woman with the wilderness eyes
Dippers and skimmers
Looking For life's Essential
Celebration
Like swirling birds inside my mind
Monuments
I look across the same land
As Ozymandias died
And see its glory
Do I lie
Quietly
Turn my speechless feet
And let it die
From a coward's heart

A shoreline washing
Standing stones
Or just old broken bones
Of some short quick-forgotten war
Its fallen men forgotten too as
We press on to certain futures
With no sacrifice Just so
Scipio
Salted Carthage
Midst a tortuous lament
And unequivocal intent
You try to sell me cheap
And cellar me for you to keep
Me trying to see the sun
Reach the light smell the blossom
Think
There's something worth the fight
I'd rather night than live
In your reductive anodyne
Inconsequential mite

Do I believe in hills
Of desiccating pulses
And Will misfortune
Countenance me
With regret
And In my late life
Shoo me on
Into my grave
Without a secret

Fragile Friends

Please don't leave me on the shelf
For if I tremble I will surely fall
And if I fall then I will surely crumble
Our fragile friends that see the sun
But only think to run and hide
The flitted butterflies that pass
So nervously alone as though they are the last
To know the moon and stars
And everybody's just like all the rest
Even the different ones
Shying from the shine
Reflecting harshly in the window panes
Or fear to plunge into their dark interiors
If I tremble If I tumble If I fall
I will surely want to lie
Where those of those tender hearts
Will bind the wounds and broken bones
And tie the bandages and sing you songs of love
And watch the birds cavort contorted
Crazy bundles in the sky

Long Ago

The alchemical quest For immortality
Was over long ago
White or graphite base lead turned to gold
Seductive words of Sappho Never growing old
No plastic overshoes can keep your feet
Forever dry
Nor silicon topcoat stay the storm
Of time's rampant weather's wither
Though its half-life last millennia Still half a life
Loving living's ecstasy your legacy
No non-biodegradable
Remains
Quality the quantity
That bears longevity
Like sighs and riffs of breathless Basho's
Rumi-nations
Van Gogh's nights
In Ludwig's Van
Leadbelly's growlin Smokestacks of Wolf Howlin
Stop by the Winehouse to
Sip some cool and heady genius
The Climb up to the superstars is short
And no stone hearts allowed
Or sour visage
Just claims to stake
To live upon Not dwell upon
The differences we make

Magnet

Like a magnet to my ferrous soul
The river draws me down
Like the stream that falls from mountain tops
That rills through rock so hard to turn a mason's gouge
And trills the ripples light over frivolous
Shallower dreams delights
To stop right where the sunlight
Sparkles There
For my eyes only
Cracks my mind
Wide open In the distance
I can hear the sound of breaking hearts And wonder
If one's mine It seems so far away now
Either beauty or bereft
Obscure your vision or it shone
For what I see is mine alone And you don't need to be
Along
Side But I'm happy if I ever see you
Shine

Grave Vigil

I mean no harm
To bring a little sadness
To this day A brief
Reflection to remember
When we bring ourselves
To arms For reasons
That delude us As
Reason does elude us Is
That not madness Just
A reflection on sadness For
Every little life that's tossed
Away Too had a little dream To set
Adrift upon the ocean
Lost ...

Masked Fluid Truth

I am Tiresias, tender as the evening
Fluid as the rendering of all
Things Liquid as a cat
An octopus of tentacles that never end
Blind as love and justice
To the false light
All seeing in the night I know
You and me And All
That we will be
From all things that we come
And to all things we will return
That which we owe
All truth unmasked
Ere fall eternal shadow

Knife edge

Reckless ways wild days a profligate haze
They say a noise to let just pass on by
While you can lash yourself to masts
On Sailing ships in rutting seas
To slash a swathe Through heaving swells
And towering waves
Like mighty devious Ulysses
To leave the rest to stop their ears
To symphonies of darkness
And listen to the Siren's Cry
A song a feeling
To resist
A feeble posturing
Like pissing
On an elephant's sting
No fear the vagabond rogue inside
The anodyne's no horse to ride
Across the wasteland
Feel the blade in
All its sharp and stunning glide
No Morpheus eyes, these
Wide Open
Under the night
When moon's the only light
That glints along the edge of reason
As it cuts
Its profile recognised
One Razor fang to draw you in
Will turn its face, a glimpse and
Two To make you sin

Dragons in the Rain

My Dragons break on savage petals
Blown along on winter
Harbinger winds
If they be real then
Let the mountains burn to light the sky And
Let their fiery breath consume me
In the flames of my indifference
If I have let my passion
Let my ardour slide
Into an apathy of
Blood diluted
Quenched emotionless in pixelated mud
A blackening of heart
Even dragons in the rain may
Spark a blaze
And when the ashes then are woke
Let them be glad that they are dust
To make again

Rich

With feet to walk a cold indifferent shore
Ocean waves
That rumble
Tumble on regardless
Of the footprints washed away so cruel a day
No country for the Beauty Kings and Queens
But salt-lashed birds
That dress their care more keenly
Keep their friendship dear
Into the eyes of storm and harsh resistance
Breakers of the freezing unkind seas
And live within their honesty
Such soaring into teeth of wind's adversity
And fly as one until the very ends of their existence

Not mine to wish I had my white wings
Fly me to oblivion
For it is not my
Turn, this life around

But while I stand
Between
The seagulls' fondness shared on February's
Chill uncaring tides
And the innocents' innocence buried in the burning sand
With all beside Their little dreams
Come, kiss me, for your luck, and know
I know I am a very fortunate man

Precious

We'll waste
No precious sunrise
Hurling anger at the sky
Throwing rocks
To stop the tide
Let's take turns
To have our backs
Towards the sun
Wherever we lie
And you know
That I will stay
With you ...
But only till I die

Icarus Recalled

Icarus told me just before he fell
Don't wail for me
It didn't matter
I got this far
The flight was all
Now straight to Hell
With ichor
Fiery liquor
Burning in my veins
And in my soul

#haiku

My heart is broken
The sea that kissed the shore now
Crashes onto sand

But on the horizon It still touches the sky

Adjacencies of
Black and blue and hue of grey
And still to soar above

Like fragile roses
Fickle friends drop their bloom but
Always keep the thorn

Reckless Pangloss

If I have been
Reckless
With my days
Wandered years
In spaced-out wastelands
Endured
Psyche's damage
Worn its illness and its fears
My muddle now appears
In its propriety

My eyes in tired sobriety
Cannot locate the point
At which its value we pursue
Followed virtue
Out of the shadow of the valley of death
And its sodden heavy veil of
Bitter tears
Yet
The watercourse on Io
Can't run down to Timbuktu
In hunger, thirst starvation's bombs
And drone strike's burst
Pangloss still shouting from the grave
This is
The possible best
And not the worst?

So sweet sister tequila
Be my friend again
Well find a joint and we
Can
Powder noses
Frequently
Till my raddled body get subsumed by dirt
While mob cruelty
Insanity
Prevail
I'll rhyme combust unjust with dust
Just because I can
And we shall hang another monkey
For a Frenchman

Risk

Our lives held
By tenuous threads
That risk that dare
To walk the clifftop
Tread the edge
While seams rip
Beneath our feet
The fissures crack
Our fragile grip
Can only be
Enheartened by
Our poesie
And some already fallen
Sad to see
Remember
Some to grieve
And others, well
Compassion be our creed
Let flocks of birds
And the autumn sun
Gather
In valediction
As they make to leave

Senses

I can
See
The sunrise
Smell the ocean
Swell
Hear cicadas
In the trees
Roil
And seethe
I can
Reach out to
Touch the moonlight
Taste my love
Lucky me
Lucky man
Lucky day

Michael J Wood

Mornings,
Cats,
& Coffee

Howling at the words
The moon appropriates me
Day breaks in darkness

91

Pink and the Cat

Pink and the cat pretend they just don't care
And turn their backs as spirits
Overstayed the night pass on their way
To catch the twilight speedily departing
Early rising Sun
A hostage to the follies
Lights upon the leaves
Momentarily
A golden tangle
Freshly woke Held Captive in the trees
Till it can wipe the sleep out of its eyes
Sounds of awakening
Seagulls bring a scent of shore
An ocean's flood A mind's
A summer's day
An Ocean of cacophony
To screel the new day in through ancient doors
And all the raucous birds begin
An Orchestra preparing
Scratching strings
And squeaking valves and hammers
On the timpani skins
Before the maestro taps the music stand
And strikes the baton through the air
Opening notes of tonic harmony
Tempo Pluck and Stroke and Exhaled breath
A rising symphony

Screech

Just That
Early morning
Rising of the cat
And coffee steam Upon the stoop
Sun the old retainer
Wipes away the mist and dew
Raucous screech of vigilant rooks
Protective of their fledging clutch
Not the prettiest sound around Engaging
Battle on the airwaves
Versus boom-cooed rock-doves
On the radio Revered
Mr Attenborough
Speaks
Of screeching
Swifts Who fly 500 miles
A day to feed their needs
The cries of life
For life Sometimes
It takes a noisy crow To
Let everybody know They're not alone
And that's a kind of peace

Morning Coffee, Morning Cats #haiku

Remnants of the night
Lingering in fey cobwebs
Coffee's cure dispels

New day's Sun comes up
Like love in a broken heart
Waiting for embrace

Woke into darkness
No fear for light day begins
Coffee plays the sun

Cat leaps to catch in
Spiral twists the last bird
Bare branches set it free

Dawn with gentle breath
Whispers thanks to fallen leaves
Life without regret

See eagle dawn rise
Devour night's querulous beasts
Give heart to the day

Doorstep Nights

>Me and Cat
>(Cat and Eye)
>Sat
>After midnight
>Late night
>Doorstep chat
>(Mostly me though, well, She does
>Occasionally Mewl)
>Smoke a cigarette
>(Me, that is)
>She strongly
>Shows her
>Dis
>Approval

>>The darkness
>>Holds us both enthralled Seductress
>>Music of the night
>>So soft the
>>Spirits of the trees
>>Gentle
>>Sighing on the breeze
>>Lamenting
>>Wistful threnodies
>>What dismal science
>>Slumbering friends
>>Are these
>>To so forget
>>The willing gifts
>>That I bequeath

#haiku

Silhouettes of trees
Crack open the darkest skies
Ready for the sun

        Chrysanthemum dawn
        Cloud fingers soft as lovers dreams
        Thank the gentle night

Cat becomes herself
Lying in the sun-seared lea
Watching crickets fly

        So as I linger
        Kitty breaks my sombre mood
        Like taste of ginger

Creation talks

Morning walks
All creation talks
Only need
To listen to
All the brave
Along the windswept wave
If I could talk the wind then I would tell you
Even the howling in the halyards has a story
To sing
Of higher skies
And I will take my freedom on the wing
Though it pass over empty shores
And keep my judgement close
Inside my maw
Careless of a scathing claw
For warm or cold the flood tide will return
Replenished riches

The Book of Tears

Michael J Wood

Seasons

Drifts of light
Rain
Drift in on sunrise'
Light
Drifts
Of leaves drift on the wind
Say drifts of snow
To follow
Drift in
Words and wine
And frozen furrow
Drift in the rain
Again
Drift in the swallow
With the rising sun
Drift into summer ...
Drift ...

Blue-sky Thinking

Sunshine's short sweet reign
Enter like a tender love too infrequently
The warm Spring hungry trees
Share their shadows Stitch
Fine filigrees
Across my vision To bewitch
While Winters weary remnants
Wait to fall into their rest ...

Leafless silhouettes
Crack skies like Monday morning's
Interrupted dreams

April 1st - *No Joke*

(Written on being invited by a local church official at 7am to join him in the chapel for breakfast bubbly – wonderful!)

    Early morning walking once again
    A little rain
    And the pretty-paint remains of the great egg hunt
    No shame, St Peter
    And St Paul quite evidently have none
    Nor the vicar any qualms
    About to cross my palms
    With bubbly, and the buds, no wiser,
    Look up to the Heavens Where
    The seagulls mob the heron There'll be
    No Buck's Fizz welcome there So
    Glad to see St Peter's Well
    And where the rest of us must go
    The rocks and ruins of Avalon
    The buoys that look like armadillos
    All the muddy shore along
    So cold my bitter fingers sting
    And halyards slap the masts so noisily In
    The chilling breeze Yet still the colours run
    Run like the rivulets forever happy babbling
    Come rain or sun There'll always be a stream to follow

Bleak Midwinter (2017)

Now the old year out and
Yes, though slow, the days grow
Still the snow
Still the cold to come
And still some gift days
Mari Lywds And Hogmanays
And Dog days yet
In the Land of Ancient Dragon's breath
To celebrate in any ways
You choose
Witch ever Magic you pursue
The present wrapped our bodies wrapped, some rapt
Some still alive unrapt and
Naked on a hostile path
Waiting for the rapture
May your meat be meet and your impish feet
Stay warm against the hearth
The Eves of little dreams have come
But don't forget the ones
For whom
Midwinter may be bleaker
Than the executioner's drum

Magic

In my dour sobriety
I am aware
What particle physi-
Fusion-chemi-
Quantum-astróno-
Colonoscopy
Has done for me
But I'm not one for splitting hares
And in my hours
My moments when I know the world
From outside in
And all its skin Naked to the sky
Scorched by fire and chill of Heaven and Hell
Of summer heat and winter's ice
Upon my back upon my face
Come near to sear my spirit
And I walk uninhibit among them
In soft and savage caress of love
And the wind blows spaces in my head
That fill with wonder, ecstasy
I know that it can only be
Magic

Grey November

Grey November Grey the sea
Grey the sky
And grey like ocean mist
To close around me Slow
The seabirds drift
To find eternity Or rest
Their frail autonomy Among the washed up husks
That Fill the pools And line along the shore
And still find time for lovers games
And others pain ...

Grey Wolf

Be pleased the seasons Know Their reason
Dishonesty The only treason
Sweet scented clover Will bring the bees
To the cherry flower
And Winter's thankless freeze Forsaken
Will be over No despair
Will keep the sun from rising
Nor the Grey-Wolf Wind From howling through the trees

Micro-Climates

Little falls
That does not rise again
Leaves Woman Snow and Rain
Let empires seeking to possess
Lie in their ruins vain
        (ackn. – Percy Bysshe Shelley, Ozymandias)

Solstice

Today's dark corners
Now surrender to the light
And softly let their places
Be caressed to life

#haiku

If gentle rain should
Kiss my face I shall call it
Grace and kiss right back

Rose evening's fall calls
Rooks and ravens to their roost
And tomorrow's sun

In a season when
Flowers lose the strength to live
And the trees slumber

Emerald green, high tarns
Impenetrable as death
Wait unfrozen yet

Butterflies

Stay still and take the
Autumn rays my pretty friends
Your work is almost done

Black Clouds

Maybe the storm rolls in
Like grim rapacious
Agamemnon's men
On a Rosy-fingered dawn
Across the wine-dark sea
And it may rant and rage
Like howling combatants
Cassandra's unheard pleas
And I stand naked on the plain
With outstretched arms
Begging the black clouds
Pour on me

Without rain

Like riveters' hammers
At my window
Need the clamour
To crack back into me
Yearning longing
Rain
Can't be without the rain
Crashing in my ears
Let it wash away the silence
Till it wash away the pain
Till it starts to feel the same
As it did before the storm passed by
And left life at a standstill
In the eye
Left me marooned
And I cannot get away
Release me back to entropy
My raging winds
Where all the burning souls begin
For whom the turn of days was made
The seasons and the changes ring
From holiness to sin

Epilogue

A Bit about #folklore

One of the Twitter #hashtags I am addicted to (did I mention I had an addictive personality?) is #FolkloreThursday. As the name suggests, tweeters are encouraged to post examples of folklore, mythology, urban myth and legend, local traditional custom relevant to a weekly theme. And there are some wonderful tales out there of grand design and everyday magic …

Laurel and Hardy – A Prose Poem (ish)
… And One of the best cinematic gags ever! ✦

June 2018

SynchronicityConnectivityCoincidence
-Laurel & Hardy #1

Ever since last week's theme for the utterly fabulous (see what I did there?) #FolkloreThursday - a world of infinite wonder it must be said - I'd been looking for a shoe in for one of my favourite movie moments; of course, I could have just tweeted the clip, but where's the fun in that?

Last week's #FolkloreThursday theme was "birthdays, anniversaries and celebrations"*, which brought forth the response of the nursery rhyme of* 'Solomon Grundy - born on a Monday …'*, etc, which triggered in my memory a smile.*

For this week's #FolkloreThursday theme of cities and urban spaces, in the immediate absence of folkloric mischief concerning Stan & Ollie, I tweeted the legend of Spring-Heeled Jack, a tale from Victorian London; and kept looking …

SynchronicityConnectivityCoincidence
-Laurel & Hardy #2

... Eventually I found the story I was looking for.

In January this year, a ghosthunter ★ photographed and spoke with the spirit of Stan Laurel in a derelict cinema in Bishop Auckland in the north of England, Stan's childhood home.

"I'm at peace," said Stan, "this is where I belong."

Sadly, I was too late to post for #FolkloreThursday.

I was tired, I fell asleep, maybe into a dream ...

However, every cloud has a silver lining, and a silver screen it seems because, most interestingly for me, during the course of research, I discovered that Solomon Grundy, whose biography instigated the whole thing, was a DC Comic World villain (I know, right? How out of touch with popular culture is that!), in particular, in Gotham, where he would have run up against ... guess who ?

I had known of the legend of Spring-Heeled Jack since schoolyard boys' talk, but I had never known until Thursday that he was the inspiration for ...

... Batman! (according to some) ...

SynchronicityConnectivityCoincidence
-Laurel & Hardy #3

SynchronicityConnectivityCoincidence
-Laurel & Hardy #3

What possible further evidence could be required in support of a Unified Field Theory, and how did Solomon Grundy lead us there?

Just ask yourself the question 'What did he die of?'

Answer: 'I think he died of a Tuesday'

And there's no need to go to Mars, except for pleasure, naturally
Of course, it could all just be coincidence

Never lie to the universe,
It's listening

The Book of Tears

ACKNOWLEDGEMENTS

Images

i. ©jreedy – photography/images
ii. ©michaeljwood – photography/images
iii. https://pixabay.com/
iv. public domain

Words

i. Casablanca (Bogart & Bergman)
ii. Homer
iii. Laurel & Hardy
- ✦ https://www.youtube.com/watch?v=96po3FRJ9uk
- ★ The Northern Echo
iv. Percy Bysshe Shelley
v. Shakespeare
vi. Susan Sontag

Song/Lyric references

i. Al Stewart *
ii. Edith Piaf
iii. Janis Ian
iv. New Order
v. Steven Stills

All the hapless huggable (and the unhapless unhuggable too, why not) #tweeters and #MerryPromptsters

#DimpleVerse
#hangtenstories
#inkMine
#IntrigueVerse
#microprompt
#PoemTrail
#SlapDashSat
#ThruLineThurs
#WIPitWED
#WrittenRiver

are a few of the #hashtags I've been delighted to use, and there are many others available through a variety of writing #prompt lists, as well as the use of #hashtags such as #writing #writerslife #nature #poetry #micropoetry #poetrycommunity whether as discrete effort, exercise or inspiration, all good …

Michael J Wood

The Book of Tears

Printed in Great Britain
by Amazon